HIDING IN PLAIN SIGHT

My Chronicle of Humanity

Guinevere Dolton

Bigtree

To all who think outside the box

CONTENTS

PREFACE

Sharing this journal, a fragment of the chronicles I have so diligently maintained, is an act both daring and fraught with doubt. For eons, I have watched your kind, humanity, as an unseen observer bound by a duty to record, not to intervene.

To reveal even a fraction of what I know feels like the unraveling of a tightly guarded tapestry, stitched together with threads of moments that shaped your species' trajectory. I am Vaelor, chronicler of the Zepharite High Council. As I pen this down, I am acutely aware of the gravity of my choice. This is not the entirety of my record; if it were, the world as you know it might crumble under the weight of truths too profound, too disruptive, to bear. I share only fragments—carefully curated glimpses into the intersections where your journey touched ours. These stories are offered not as revelations, but as reflections: mirrors that may help you better understand yourselves.

What compels me to unveil this to you? It is not vanity or hubris, but a profound hope to help. For millennia, we have debated whether knowledge should illuminate or obscure, whether revealing ourselves would inspire progress or ignite chaos. Today, I take a step toward illumination, knowing full well the risk that accompanies it.

Yet I worry. I worry that exposing you to truths long hidden might alter the delicate balance of your progression. Your kind thrives on paradox—fragile yet resilient, destructive yet creative. What if the knowledge I share changes that dynamic? What if it accelerates your evolution in ways you are not ready for? Or worse, what if it extinguishes the spark of curiosity that defines you, replacing it with fear or complacency?

This journal is both a warning and a gift. It is a testimony to the intricate dance of observation and non-intervention, a dance that we have performed in the shadows of your history. It is a reminder that you are not alone, that the tapestry of existence is woven with threads both seen and unseen. Above all, it is an invitation: to reflect, to question, and to strive for the brilliance I have glimpsed in you, time and again.

As you read these pages, remember that this is but a sliver of the vast chronicles I hold. There are truths I dare not share, revelations that could send your world spiraling into chaos. Let this fragment be enough—for now. It is my hope that it serves as a guide, a spark, and perhaps, in time, a bridge between us.

Humanity stands on the brink of transformation, and I, too, am part of that journey. Let these chronicles remind you of the choices you make and the paths you forge, for they will shape not only your story but ours as well.

—Vaelor, Chronicler of the Zepharite High Council

CHAPTER 1

A World Unveiled

I am Vaelor, chronicler of the Zepharite High Council—a position both honored and burdened. For millennia, I have observed your kind: humanity, a species that dances precariously on the edge of brilliance and ruin. You do not know me, nor will you see me. To you, I am invisible—a shadow cloaked in advanced science, a whisper woven through your myths. Yet though unseen, we are here. We have always been here. Watching. Recording. Questioning whether your story is one of triumph or self-destruction.

Our initial encounter with your world was an accident, a serendipitous deviation from a carefully calculated course. While charting the stars, our instruments detected an anomaly: a small, vibrant planet, pulsing with life in the cold void of space. At first glance, Earth was unremarkable—a lush sphere of oceans, forests, and primitive ecosystems. But deeper scans revealed something extraordinary: a species that walked upright, crafted tools, and adapted to adversity with an ingenuity we had rarely seen.

You were fragile by the standards of advanced life. Your bodies, bound by the limits of your atmosphere, required air, water, and warmth. Yet, beneath this frailty burned a fire—a relentless drive to shape your world. It was this contradiction, this mix of vulnerability and ambition, that first drew us to you.

In your infancy, you tamed fire, shaped stone, and whispered prayers to the stars. When we set foot on your soil for the first time, around 10,000 of your Earth years ago, your kind roamed in scattered tribes. Our presence was cloaked in technology beyond your comprehension, yet one among you —a young hunter hardened by survival—stumbled upon us.

To him, we must have seemed divine. Our reflective suits glimmered faintly in the firelight as he dropped to his knees, his spear clattering to the ground. He babbled incomprehensibly, his wide eyes a mix of fear and awe. Before he could approach, we vanished, retreating to our craft. But the moment lingered.

By morning, his hands had etched crude figures of radiant beings onto the walls of his tribe's cave. We watched as his story spread, his encounter twisting into myth and legend. From that solitary moment, gods were born—figures bathed in light who came from the heavens to inspire, guide, or punish.

The incident sparked fierce debate within the High Council. Should we reveal ourselves? Share our knowledge? Guide your kind toward enlightenment? Or would our intervention stoke the flames of chaos? Humanity's capacity for creation was undeniable, but so too was your capacity for destruction. In the end, caution prevailed.

We chose observation over intervention. Over the centuries, we established hidden outposts beneath your oceans, cloaked satellites in your orbit, and emissaries within your societies. We perfected invisibility, ensuring our presence would remain undetected.

And so, we watched.

From humble beginnings, you astonished us. You formed alliances, built cities, and created monuments that defied time. When the pyramids of Giza rose, their geometric precision rivaled even our engineering feats. Their construction sparked theories among my peers. Had your kind uncovered remnants of ancient Zepharite technology? But no—the pyramids were yours, a testament to raw human brilliance.

Yet your capacity for creation was matched by your penchant for destruction. You warred over resources, power, and ideology, often reducing your achievements to ash. To us, these struggles were perplexing. Why would a species so capable of cooperation choose division? Why did your brilliance so often serve your ruin?

As centuries passed, our technology advanced. We refined our observation methods, embedding ourselves deeper into your world without leaving a trace. Occasionally, our efforts faltered—a malfunctioning drone here, a fleeting sighting there. You called them miracles, visions, or UFOs, weaving them into the tapestry of your imagination. Each time, we adapted, erasing the evidence and ensuring the patterns remained unconnected.

Your 20th century marked a perilous chapter. You split the atom, harnessing a power capable of obliterating your kind. We debated intervention as mushroom clouds darkened your skies and cities burned. Yet even in destruction, you displayed resilience. You rebuilt. You forged alliances. You sought peace. It was this paradox—your ability to rise from the ashes—that kept us watching.

Now, as your telescopes pierce the void and your machines reach for distant worlds, you stand on the cusp of a great revelation. You are unraveling the mysteries of existence, inching closer to discovering us. When that day comes, your story—and ours—will change forever.

Will you greet us with curiosity or fear? Will you embrace us as allies or lash out as adversaries? The answer, I suspect, lies in the lessons of your past.

Humanity is unique—a species of contradictions, capable of boundless creation and senseless destruction. You are a puzzle we have yet to solve. And so, we remain. Watching. Waiting. Silent witnesses to a world on the brink of transformation.

Time will tell whether your story ends in brilliance or ruin. Until then, I am here, chronicling the choices that will shape your destiny.

CHAPTER TWO

The Shaman and the Stars

Circa 10,000 BCE

The fire crackled beneath the vast, star-filled sky, its embers rising like whispers to the heavens. Kova knelt close to the flames, her bronze-toned face painted with shifting shadows. Around her, the tribe sat in expectant silence—elders leaned forward, children nestled against their parents, and hunters rested with spears laid at their sides. Kova was their shaman, the keeper of their stories, their bridge to the unknown.

But tonight, Kova had no story to tell.

Her gaze was fixed upward, where the stars gleamed brighter than ever before. They shimmered and danced in patterns she had never seen, casting faint, eerie light across the jagged cliffs that framed their settlement. Her heartbeat quickened, a question stirring within her. It was not fear, but a yearning—an ache to understand the vastness above.

Far beyond her sight, we watched.

Our vessel hovered silently in the void, its cloaking field bending light and sound around its form. My assignment was clear: observe and catalog. The Council had identified this region of early Earth as ideal for studying the interplay between primitive life and a fragile ecosystem. Humanity was a peripheral detail, a species noted for its unusual adaptability but still deemed inconsequential.

And yet, I was drawn to Kova.

She was different. Her senses were unusually sharp, her gaze unerringly following even the faintest distortion of light where our vessel shimmered in the starlight. Though she could not see us, she felt us. Her movements were purposeful, her silence laden with a weight that seemed to transcend her tribe's understanding.

The Journey to the Ridge

The stars shifted again, their light pressing down as though calling to her. Kova rose abruptly, her carved wooden staff tapping softly against the ground. She walked away from the fire, her steps steady and deliberate. The murmurs of her tribe rippled through the still air, but none dared follow. She was their shaman; if she sought answers in the dark, it was not their place to question.

I tracked her ascent from the observation deck of our vessel. Her path led her to a rocky ridge overlooking the settlement, where she halted, staring directly at the faint shimmer in the air—the cloaked outline of our craft.

She knelt, her staff slipping from her fingers to rest on the ground. Her lips moved rapidly, forming words I could not understand. Prayers? Invocations? Or perhaps questions whispered to gods she believed she had found. Her trembling hand extended toward the shimmer, brushing against the invisible boundary of the cloaking field.

Protocol dictated retreat at the first sign of detection, but I hesitated. Something in her expression—awe mingled with quiet certainty—held me in place.

The Moment of Contact

Her touch rippled faintly across the field, a sensation both tangible and intangible. Her fear melted into reverence. Her wide eyes glistened in the starlight, not with terror, but with wonder.

In that moment, I saw Kova not as a primitive anomaly but as a bridge—a mind reaching beyond its understanding to touch the unknown. She could not comprehend us, yet she accepted our presence with an almost childlike grace.

I recorded every detail: the dilation of her pupils, the shift in her posture, the rapid beats of her heart. But no metric could capture the gravity of her encounter.

By the time I withdrew the field, she had fallen into a deep silence, her trembling hand resting on the cold stone.

The Carvings and the Stories

When dawn broke, Kova returned to her people. Without a word, she took up her carving tools and etched symbols into the cliffside. Figures of light descending from the stars took shape beneath her hands, their forms radiant and otherworldly. Her tribe gathered to watch, their murmurs growing into reverent whispers.

The carvings became sacred. Kova's encounter redefined their rituals, reshaped their stories. She spoke of beings who walked among the stars, who watched and guided. Her vision gave her people a sense of purpose, a belief that they were part of something far greater.

Over centuries, her story grew into legend. The carvings weathered but endured, etched into stone and memory. They would later be discovered by archaeologists, who puzzled over their meaning. Theories of primitive astronomy and early spiritual symbolism would flourish, but none would uncover the truth.

Vaelor's Reflection

I often think of Kova.

Her life was forever changed by a moment of accidental contact. Her people revered her as a conduit to the divine, yet she remained grounded, her eyes forever searching the stars. I observed her until the end of her days, documenting how that fleeting encounter rippled outward.

Had I given her a gift, or burdened her with a mystery she could never solve? The question lingered long after she was gone.

Kova never saw us again, but the light in her eyes endured, passed down in the stories her people told and the symbols they carved. Her spark became a flame, connecting the stars above to the hearts of those below.

As I watched her legacy unfold, I realized the profound simplicity of her truth: humanity does not need to understand everything to find meaning. Sometimes, the mystery itself is enough.

CHAPTER THREE

The Engineer of Giza

Circa 2560 BCE

The sun blazed relentlessly over the sands of Egypt, casting long shadows across the plateau where thousands toiled under the weight of massive limestone blocks. Their chants echoed rhythmically, a symphony of effort and determination. Overseers barked commands, their voices harsh against the grinding of stone sledges. Above it all, Imhotep stood on a makeshift scaffold, his linen robe rippling lightly in the desert wind.

To the workers, he was the architect of the pharaoh's grand vision, a man blessed by the gods with insight beyond mortal comprehension. To himself, he was a steward of eternity. This was no mere tomb—it was a declaration, a monument that would defy time and proclaim the triumph of human ingenuity.

But to us, Imhotep was a curiosity.

Our vessel hovered silently beyond the visible spectrum, observing the construction of what you now call the Great Pyramid. The site had drawn our attention due to unique electromagnetic anomalies—the interplay between the limestone bedrock and geomagnetic fields. Yet what fascinated me most was not the structure itself but the man who commanded its creation.

Imhotep's mind shone with a brilliance that rivaled the finest architects of advanced civilizations. His grasp of mathematics, geometry, and astronomy transcended the limitations of his era. From my vantage point, I suspected there was something more—an almost preternatural understanding of harmony between the heavens and the earth.

The Storm and the Vision

The desert often turned treacherous, its stillness giving way to sudden chaos. One evening, as the workers retreated to their tents and the plateau fell into silence, a sandstorm erupted on the horizon. The winds howled like enraged spirits, and grains of sand swirled into an impenetrable vortex.

Imhotep, unshaken by the storm, climbed to the scaffold to retrieve his scrolls. His silhouette against the raging tempest was striking, a lone figure defying nature's wrath. It was then that the storm disturbed one of our reconnaissance drones, sending it plummeting toward the construction site.

The drone's cloaking mechanisms faltered for a brief moment, releasing a faint, shimmering light into the storm's chaos. Imhotep froze, shielding his eyes against the glow. His steps were deliberate as he approached, his mind undoubtedly racing to make sense of the vision before him.

From the observation deck of our vessel, I debated whether to intervene. Protocol dictated retrieval of the drone and immediate erasure of any trace of our presence. Yet Imhotep's reaction gave me pause.

His movements were not driven by fear but by reverence. He knelt, his hands trembling as he reached out, sensing the faint hum of the drone. The light reflected in his wide eyes, igniting a spark of inspiration I had never seen before. The interaction lasted mere moments before the drone stabilized and ascended back into the storm's cover, but the effect on Imhotep was indelible.

The Transformation

The morning after the storm, Imhotep returned to the construction site with a fervor that astounded even his closest aides. His sketches, refined overnight, revealed subtle yet transformative adjustments to the pyramid's design.

He realigned the structure's angles with astonishing precision, ensuring its orientation perfectly matched the cardinal points. His calculations incorporated celestial alignments, connecting the pyramid not only to the earth but to the heavens. Workers spoke in hushed tones of the divine light he had seen during the storm, attributing his insights to a revelation from the gods.

Over the following months, the Great Pyramid rose with a grace and precision that defied its time. The limestone blocks fit seamlessly, their placement suggesting an understanding of weight distribution and balance far beyond the tools and knowledge available to his people.

Imhotep's transformation rippled through the kingdom. His writings hinted at new approaches to construction, medicine, and governance, marking the dawn of innovations that would resonate across centuries. To the world, he became a legend—a figure whose accomplishments blurred the line between human ingenuity and divine inspiration.

Vaelor's Reflection

From the shadows, I documented every step of the pyramid's construction and the man behind its creation. I wondered: Had our fleeting encounter merely amplified a trajectory Imhotep was already destined to follow? Or had I interfered, altering the natural course of human development?

The Council debated my report with unusual fervor. Some saw Imhotep's achievements as a testament to humanity's innate potential, needing no intervention. Others argued that even the faintest touch could create ripples with unforeseen consequences.

For me, the answer lay in Imhotep himself. His brilliance was not born of our presence; it was his alone. Our brief interaction simply provided a lens through which he focused the light of his imagination.

The Great Pyramid endures as a marvel of human history, its mysteries captivating generations. Its purpose has been debated endlessly: a tomb, a celestial observatory, a beacon. But to me, its true significance lies in what it represents—a moment when humanity reached for eternity, guided not by tools or technology but by the boundless potential of the human mind.

Imhotep never saw the shimmering light again, but I believe he carried it with him until his final days. His legacy is not merely the stone structure that stands in the sands of Giza but the idea that creation, at its core, is an act of transcendence.

As I continue my chronicle, I often reflect on Imhotep. He reminds me that humanity's greatest achievements are not always the result of intervention but of their relentless drive to understand, to create, and to connect.

CHAPTER FOUR

The Visionary Inventor

Circa 1500 CE

The hills of Vinci basked in the golden hues of a setting sun. Wildflowers swayed gently in the breeze, filling the air with their subtle fragrance. At the edge of the woods, a young man sat on a weathered stone, sketchbook balanced on his knees. His charcoal pencil moved with an almost feverish energy, capturing the swooping arcs and delicate curves of birds in flight.

Leonardo da Vinci's sharp eyes followed the creatures as they darted through the sky. His sketches, though rough, pulsed with life, each line imbued with his longing to unravel the mysteries of motion. He had been fascinated by the notion of flight for as long as he could remember, dreaming of machines that could lift humanity into the heavens. To many in Vinci, Leonardo's ideas bordered on the absurd—whimsical musings of an eccentric genius. But to him, they were glimpses of the possible, seeds of a future that lay just beyond the grasp of his time.

Far above, unseen by mortal eyes, I watched.

Leonardo had been the focus of my observation for months. His mind, a torrent of creativity and precision, stood apart even in an era bursting with art, science, and philosophy. The Council tasked me with documenting humanity's progress during this period of Renaissance, a pivotal moment in their evolution. But Leonardo was more than a subject of study—he was a puzzle, a confluence of traits that both inspired and confounded us.

The Encounter in the Forest

On a moonless night, Leonardo ventured deeper into the woods. The air was cool, and the trees formed a shadowy canopy that seemed to press closer with each step. He carried his sketchbook and a lantern, its dim glow casting flickering shadows on the forest floor.

He was searching for inspiration, as he often did, his mind restless and eager. But this night, inspiration found him.

A malfunction in one of our atmospheric probes caused it to descend prematurely. The small, sleek craft emitted a faint hum and a soft glow as it settled in a clearing, its camouflage imperfect in the darkness.

Leonardo froze mid-step, his sharp instincts immediately attuned to the anomaly. His eyes narrowed, and he approached cautiously, the lantern trembling in his hand. As he neared the probe, its metallic surface shimmered faintly, a fusion of organic curves and angular precision.

Though startled, his fear was quickly overtaken by curiosity. He crouched beside the machine, running his fingers over its smooth exterior. His mind raced, forming hypotheses and rejecting them just as quickly. He retrieved his sketchbook and began to draw, capturing the craft's intricate details with astonishing accuracy.

I watched from above, torn between protocol and an irresistible urge to let the encounter unfold. Interference was forbidden, but Leonardo's brilliance compelled me to stay my hand. This was no ordinary human—his mind mirrored the adaptability and ingenuity of our own.

A Spark of Inspiration

As Leonardo sketched, the probe emitted a faint pulse of energy, a glitch in its systems. The pulse resonated with the surrounding air, creating a low, harmonic hum. Leonardo paused, his head tilting as he absorbed the sound. His pencil moved again, this time capturing not just the machine's form but the essence of its function.

He imagined gears and pulleys, mechanisms that could mimic the flight of birds and the grace of water. Though he did not fully understand what he saw, his mind leapt ahead, filling the gaps with intuition and ingenuity.

When the time came to retrieve the probe, I initiated the recall sequence. It rose silently into the air, its glow intensifying before it vanished into the night sky. Leonardo stumbled back, his eyes wide with wonder, clutching his sketches as though they were sacred relics. He stayed in the clearing long after the probe was gone, his thoughts undoubtedly racing with questions.

The Renaissance of Ideas

The encounter left a lasting mark on Leonardo. In the weeks that followed, he retreated to his workshop, driven by a newfound intensity. He refined his designs for flying machines, incorporating elements that hinted at an understanding of aerodynamics far beyond his time.

His notebooks, already brimming with ideas, swelled with new concepts. He sketched wings that mimicked birds' flight and mechanisms that could propel humanity into the skies. He delved into studies of water, motion, and anatomy with a precision that bordered on obsession.

To his contemporaries, these creations were fascinating but impractical, dismissed as the dreams of an eccentric mind. Yet, centuries later, they would inspire engineers, scientists, and visionaries who would turn his dreams into reality.

Vaelor's Reflection

From the shadows, I observed Leonardo's relentless pursuit of understanding. He reminded me of the best qualities of humanity—boundless curiosity, resilience in the face of ignorance, and an unquenchable thirst for knowledge. His encounter with the probe had not given him answers; it had sparked questions that drove him to explore the limits of his imagination.

The Council reprimanded me for allowing the incident to occur, citing the potential for contamination of their natural development. But I argued that Leonardo's brilliance was his own. The probe had merely been a catalyst, amplifying a trajectory he was already destined to follow.

Even now, I wonder if Leonardo ever questioned the origin of the machine he encountered in the woods. Perhaps he dismissed it as a fleeting vision, a figment of his vivid imagination. Or perhaps he saw it for what it truly was: a glimpse into the unknown, a doorway to the possible.

Leonardo da Vinci's legacy endures not because of what he built but because of what he envisioned. His work reminds us that humanity's greatest achievements are born not from certainty but from the audacity to dream.

As I continue my chronicle, I often return to Leonardo's story. He was a man of his time, yet he saw far beyond it. In him, I saw the spark that defines your kind—the relentless pursuit of the impossible, the willingness to reach for the stars even when bound to the earth.

CHAPTER FIVE

The Coder of Shadows

Circa 1942 CE

The damp chill of an English autumn crept into the dimly lit halls of Bletchley Park. Outside, a faint mist clung to the ivy-covered walls, muffling the distant echoes of wartime. Inside, Clara Morgan sat hunched over her workbench, her breath visible in the cool air. The rhythmic click of the Enigma decryption machine blended with the faint hum of generators, the soundtrack of an invisible war.

Clara's sharp eyes darted over the intercepted German communications before her. Lines of seemingly indecipherable code filled the pages, each sequence a puzzle begging to be unraveled. She was one of the many brilliant minds recruited to crack the Enigma cipher, yet she worked largely in the shadows. As a woman in a field dominated by men, her contributions often went unacknowledged. Still, she persisted, her determination fueled not by recognition but by the conviction that her work could change the tide of the war.

From the cloaked vantage of my vessel, I watched.

The Second World War was a paradox, showcasing humanity's capacity for both ingenuity and destruction. The Council had dispatched me to observe this era, a crucible of technological advancement born from desperation. Clara's mind stood out—a rare combination of intuition and intellect, capable of weaving coherence from chaos.

The Disturbance

One stormy evening, Clara lingered in the lab long after her colleagues had gone. Rain lashed against the windows, and thunder rumbled distantly as she bent over a particularly complex string of ciphertext. Something about the pattern tugged at her intuition, but exhaustion clouded her focus.

Suddenly, the lights flickered, and the room was plunged into darkness. A low hum filled the air as the backup generator kicked in, bathing the lab in a faint blue glow. Clara froze, her instincts sharp despite her fatigue.

The glow, however, wasn't coming from the emergency lights.

In the far corner of the room, faint symbols shimmered in the air, their intricate patterns shifting like liquid silver. Unbeknownst to Clara, the anomaly was caused by one of our cloaked drones malfunctioning nearby. The device's cloaking field faltered briefly, creating a distortion that bled into the room's electromagnetic environment.

Clara approached cautiously, her notebook clutched tightly in one hand. The symbols were unlike anything she had seen, their shapes both geometric and organic, as if they carried meaning beyond human comprehension.

The Breakthrough

Though wary, Clara's fear gave way to fascination. She retrieved a pencil and began sketching the patterns, her strokes quick and precise. She analyzed the shimmering forms as though they were another cipher, her mind racing to decipher their structure.

The drone's cloaking mechanisms stabilized, and the symbols vanished as abruptly as they had appeared. Clara stood in stunned silence, her notebook filled with meticulous sketches. The anomaly, though fleeting, ignited a spark in her mind.

Over the following weeks, Clara worked tirelessly. Inspired by the symbols, she began devising new approaches to the Enigma code. She identified patterns others had overlooked, her insights accelerating the decryption of critical German messages. Her breakthroughs allowed Allied forces to anticipate U-boat movements and bombing campaigns, saving countless lives.

Clara attributed her success to a late-night burst of inspiration, unaware of the extraterrestrial origin of the anomaly that had shaped her thinking.

The Legacy of Shadows

Though her contributions remained classified for decades, Clara's work was pivotal. Historians would later uncover her notebooks, their pages filled with enigmatic sketches that puzzled cryptographers and mathematicians alike. Some dismissed the symbols as creative flourishes, while others speculated about their meaning.

For me, the incident raised questions about the boundaries of observation. The Council chastised my failure to retrieve the malfunctioning drone, citing the potential contamination of human development. Yet I could not help but marvel at Clara's response. Her brilliance had not been gifted by us— it was hers alone. The anomaly had simply illuminated a path she was already poised to follow.

Clara Morgan never knew the true nature of the shimmering symbols that sparked her inspiration. To her, they were a puzzle, another challenge in a life defined by problem-solving. Yet her work left an indelible mark on history, advancing the science of cryptography and laying the foundation for modern computing.

Vaelor's Reflection

From the shadows, I observed Clara's quiet brilliance. She was a beacon of resilience in a world often indifferent to her contributions. Her story reminded me that humanity's strength lies not in perfection but in its capacity to adapt and innovate.

The Council debated whether my failure to retrieve the drone constituted interference. I argued that Clara's success was inevitable. The anomaly had not given her answers—it had revealed new questions, and she had answered them with the full force of her intellect.

Even now, I wonder if Clara ever sensed the anomaly's origin. Perhaps she dismissed it as a quirk of exhaustion or an atmospheric disturbance. Or perhaps, deep in her subconscious, she recognized it as a fleeting touch of something greater.

Her legacy endures, woven into the fabric of human progress. Clara Morgan's work was not just a triumph of intellect but a testament to the quiet determination of those who labor in the shadows. She reminds me that the smallest spark can illuminate the darkest moments, guiding humanity toward its boundless potential.

CHAPTER SIX

The Architect of Cryptos

Circa 2008 CE

The world was unraveling. In the wake of the 2008 global financial crisis, trust in institutions—banks, governments, corporations—shattered like glass. Entire economies buckled, and the weight of their collapse bore down on ordinary people. Savings evaporated overnight. Homes were lost. Dreams dissolved. Amid the chaos, whispers of discontent grew louder, questioning the systems that had failed them.

In the shadows of this upheaval, a spark ignited. It began as a quiet voice on a cryptographic forum, proposing an idea as radical as it was profound. A name accompanied it: Satoshi Nakamoto.

Far above, cloaked in the vastness of space, I watched.

Humanity's reliance on centralized systems had long intrigued the Council. They had persisted for centuries, despite their inherent fragility. The 2008 crash marked a turning point, a moment when the fragility of these systems was laid bare. Satoshi's proposal, though unassuming at first glance, caught my attention. It was more than an idea; it was a revolution encoded in mathematics.

The Birth of the Blockchain

Satoshi's concept was elegantly simple yet profoundly disruptive. A decentralized digital currency, unbound by governments or banks, operating on a transparent ledger that no single entity could control. The blockchain.

To the world, it was a technological innovation. To me, it was a reflection of universal principles—resilience, decentralization, and trustless collaboration. These were ideas my species had perfected long ago, woven into the fabric of our interstellar networks.

As I monitored the early communications surrounding Satoshi's proposal, I detected patterns in their design that mirrored the quantum algorithms of Zepharite systems. This alignment fascinated me. Was it coincidence, or had humanity reached a stage of development where its brightest minds began converging on universal truths?

The Silent Adjustment

Despite its brilliance, Satoshi's original code contained inefficiencies—flaws that, left unchecked, could have rendered the blockchain vulnerable to manipulation. Observing this, I made a decision that would haunt me later. Through an imperceptible manipulation of the system's electromagnetic environment, I introduced subtle adjustments to the code. These modifications strengthened the blockchain's resilience, ensuring its scalability and integrity for the challenges to come. To Satoshi and the community, these changes appeared as natural iterations, the product of collective refinement. But they were not entirely human in origin.

The first Bitcoin block—the Genesis Block—was mined in January 2009. Encoded within it was a message: *"The Times 03/Jan/2009 Chancellor on brink of second bailout for banks."* It was a quiet declaration of defiance, a symbol of the distrust that birthed the system.

The Movement Grows

Bitcoin's early days were quiet, its network sustained by a small group of cryptographic enthusiasts. But as the cracks in traditional systems widened, the currency gained traction. It was more than a medium of exchange; it became a symbol of liberation, a way to transact without intermediaries or oversight.

The blockchain's applications quickly expanded beyond currency. It became the foundation for decentralized systems in finance, governance, and supply chains. Satoshi

Nakamoto's vision extended further than even they could have imagined.

And then, as suddenly as they had appeared, Satoshi vanished.

Their last communication came in 2011. Speculation about their identity spiraled into legend. Were they an individual? A collective? A ghost in the machine? For me, the answer was clear: Satoshi Nakamoto was human, driven by the same blend of frustration, curiosity, and ingenuity that defines your species.

The Ripple Effects

Over time, the blockchain evolved, inspiring innovations that reshaped entire industries. It challenged entrenched power structures, presenting a vision of a world where trust could be decentralized and corruption minimized. Yet it also brought unforeseen consequences: environmental concerns from energy-intensive mining, speculative bubbles that enriched a few while bankrupting others, and the misuse of anonymity for illicit activities.

From my vantage point, I saw both promise and peril. Humanity's ability to adapt this tool to its highest ideals—or its darkest impulses—would determine the blockchain's legacy.

Vaelor's Reflection

The Council reprimanded me for my subtle interference. They argued that even the smallest adjustments could lead to unintended consequences. But I stood by my actions. The blockchain's resilience had ensured its survival in a world fraught with volatility.

Even now, I wonder if Satoshi ever sensed the anomalies in their system. Did they pause, however briefly, to marvel at the elegance of their creation? Or did they attribute its robustness entirely to their vision and the collective efforts of their peers?

The impact of Satoshi's work endures, rippling far beyond the cryptocurrency it birthed. Blockchain technology has become a foundation for humanity's ambitions, enabling new forms of collaboration, transparency, and trust.

To me, Satoshi Nakamoto represents the best of your kind—a willingness to challenge the status quo, to build something better from the ruins of what came before. Their legacy is not just a system of code but a testament to humanity's ability to adapt and evolve in the face of crisis.

The blockchain is humanity's first step toward systems that mirror the interstellar networks we perfected long ago. It is a reminder that even in the darkest moments, a single idea can illuminate a path forward.

And so, I remain, watching as your kind continues to reach for the future, one block at a time.

CHAPTER SEVEN

The Creator of Light

Circa 2022 CE

The early morning light filtered through the thick trees, casting long shadows over the ground. The air was cool and damp, the silence of the forest punctuated only by the occasional rustle of leaves. Amidst this stillness, a figure moved with purpose, his mind far from the natural beauty surrounding him. He was an inventor, a dreamer, a creator—Nikola Tesla.

Tesla walked with his usual deliberate pace, head slightly lowered, eyes locked on the ground as though he were searching for answers buried in the earth itself. His mind, however, was light-years away, caught in the threads of ideas that danced like lightning through his consciousness.

I had been observing Tesla for months, intrigued by the complexity of his thoughts and the scope of his ambitions. His vision was vast—he sought to change the world, to provide energy freely, to bring light to every corner of humanity. But there was something more to him. Something hidden beneath the surface.

The Moment of Revelation

One evening, Tesla sat in his laboratory, a small, cluttered space filled with coils, wires, and unfinished inventions. The hum of electricity crackled in the air as he carefully adjusted a circuit. His eyes gleamed with intensity, his fingers moving with practiced precision. Yet, there was a quiet desperation to his movements, a sense that something important was just beyond his grasp.

The laboratory door creaked open, and a sudden gust of wind caused the candles on the workbench to flicker. Tesla turned sharply, his senses immediately alert. But there was no one in the doorway. Only the faintest shimmer in the air

—an anomaly, barely perceptible but unmistakable. It was a signal, something beyond the natural world.

Tesla's heart raced. He reached for the nearest object—an iron rod—and held it out, as though he were warding off an invisible presence. His eyes widened, searching the room for any sign of the source. The shimmer flickered again, this time more distinct, emanating from the corner of the room where a coil of wire sat untouched.

The Encounter with the Unknown

What happened next was more profound than any of Tesla's previous encounters with electricity. The energy in the room seemed to concentrate, gathering in the air, crackling with a power Tesla had never experienced. A faint hum filled the space, and for a brief moment, Tesla felt himself connected to something much greater than himself. The shimmer in the air expanded, revealing itself as something more—an otherworldly presence, invisible but tangible.

Tesla stepped forward, his hand trembling slightly as he reached out to touch the electric coil. The moment his fingers made contact, a surge of energy coursed through him, unlike anything he had ever felt. His body arced with electricity, and the room around him seemed to distort, the walls bending as if reality itself were giving way.

He cried out in astonishment—not from pain, but from the sheer intensity of the experience. The surge of energy was not just physical; it was mental, spiritual, transcendent. Tesla's mind raced, a torrent of thoughts and ideas flooding in, each more extraordinary than the last. He saw visions of a world illuminated by free energy, where electricity was no longer bound by wires, but could flow freely through the air, uncontained by the traditional systems that governed it.

For a brief moment, he believed he understood it all—the nature of the universe, the secret that had eluded him for so long. He saw the future, a future where humanity could tap into the boundless energy of the earth and the stars. It was a vision of possibility, a dream of a world where no one would suffer from scarcity or darkness.

But then, as quickly as it had come, the energy receded. The room fell silent again, the hum fading into the distance. Tesla was left standing alone, trembling, his mind reeling from the encounter.

The Aftermath

For days, Tesla could not shake the feeling that something had changed within him. His mind, once focused solely on the practical application of energy, now overflowed with concepts that seemed almost too grand to be real. He could no longer merely work within the boundaries of conventional physics; his thoughts reached beyond the known, toward something that defied all understanding.

He resumed his work, but his inventions became increasingly unconventional. He spoke of wireless energy transmission, of tapping into the ether and pulling energy directly from the air. Yet, with each new idea, Tesla's work became more eccentric, his reputation more controversial.

He never spoke of the encounter in his laboratory again. To him, it was a private revelation, a moment of divine insight that he could never fully articulate to others. And yet, it haunted him—this feeling that the forces of nature he had long sought to harness were, in fact, beyond his comprehension. That what he had touched that night was not simply electricity, but a glimpse into a reality far greater than any invention could contain.

Vaelor's Reflection

From my position, I observed Tesla's transformation with a mixture of fascination and trepidation. The energy he had encountered was not of his world, and yet it had stirred something deep within him. I had allowed the anomaly to unfold, for it seemed a necessary catalyst for his work, though it risked altering the trajectory of his inventions.

The Council debated my actions, questioning whether the encounter had tipped the balance in favor of unchecked advancement. They argued that humanity's path should be dictated by their own intellectual and scientific rigor. But I knew the truth: Tesla's brilliance was not a product of mere observation. It was born from a deep connection with the mysteries of the universe, a connection that we had allowed him to glimpse.

Tesla never fully understood what had occurred that night in his laboratory, but it shaped the course of his life. His contributions to electricity and energy were monumental, but it was the spirit of his vision—the belief that energy could be free, unchained, and limitless—that would resonate through history long after his death.

Nikola Tesla's legacy is not simply in the machines he built or the patents he secured. His true gift to humanity was the vision he left behind—a vision that continues to inspire those who seek to harness the untapped forces of nature, and to dream of a world illuminated by the infinite possibilities of the universe.

And as I continue my chronicles, I am reminded that the greatest discoveries often come not from the search for answers, but from the willingness to reach into the unknown. Tesla reached out into the void and touched something greater than himself. It was a moment of transcendence, one that will echo through humanity's future.

CHAPTER EIGHT

The Digital Maverick

Circa 2027 CE

The room pulsed with a dim, cold light emanating from an array of monitors, their screens an intricate mosaic of shifting code. Streams of encrypted data cascaded down, an endless digital waterfall defying comprehension. Malik Jafari, known in the shadowy echelons of the digital world as Specter, sat motionless, his face illuminated by the flickering glow. Every keystroke was a calculated strike, every line of code a weapon in his silent war against injustice.

Malik's name was a legend whispered among hackers—not for greed or power but for his crusade against corruption and control. His targets were chosen with surgical precision: corporations thriving on exploitation, regimes suppressing dissent, and systems designed to enslave the powerless. Yet tonight's mission was unlike any before. His adversary was not a single entity but a hidden global surveillance network —an unholy alliance of nations wielding control in the shadows. Malik thrived under pressure, his resolve steeled against the stakes. But tonight, he was not alone in his crusade.

Beyond human comprehension, in realms of abstract light and energy, Vaelor observed. Among the Zepharites, Earth had long been a source of curiosity, a theater of boundless potential and contradictions. While his kin watched humanity from afar, detached and clinical, Vaelor had always seen something extraordinary. In Malik Jafari, he saw an echo of the Zepharites' own adaptability and defiance. This human, driven by an unyielding sense of justice, fascinated him.

Vaelor's intervention was delicate, an artful nudge rather than overt interference. To aid Malik, he seeded the algorithms Malik encountered with enhancements—improvements imperceptible to human senses yet profound in their effect. Malik remained unaware of the alien hand guiding his work, his focus unbroken as he delved deeper into the labyrinthine code of the surveillance network.

As the night deepened, Malik's monitors began to display anomalies. Strange symbols flickered within the code—elegant, intricate shapes that defied programming logic. At first, Malik dismissed them as glitches, remnants of corrupted data. But the symbols persisted, their patterns impossible to ignore. Intrigued, Malik isolated the anomalies and ran them through his decryption tools.

The result was astonishing: an impossibly detailed map of connections and vulnerabilities. It was a schematic that exposed not just the surveillance network but the very foundations of global power. Malik's heart raced as he traced the lines of the map, each discovery both exhilarating and terrifying. The complexity of the data exceeded anything human ingenuity could produce, yet Malik's resolve was unshaken. He pressed on, navigating the network with a skill that bordered on superhuman, his tools subtly enhanced by Vaelor's unseen guidance.

Hours passed in a blur of keystrokes and revelations. Files began to surface—evidence implicating governments, corporations, and clandestine organizations in an unprecedented conspiracy of control. The revelations were seismic, and Malik knew he was no longer working in the shadows.

The fallout was swift and explosive. Within days, news outlets were flooded with stories of mass surveillance and manipulation. Governments scrambled to contain the outrage, but the truth could not be suppressed. Activists and whistleblowers hailed Specter as a hero, while the world reeled from the implications of his actions. True to his reputation, Malik vanished from the digital landscape as quickly as he had emerged, leaving no trace.

Yet the impact of Malik's work went far beyond his immediate victories. The collapse of the surveillance network ignited a global movement. Grassroots initiatives began advocating for decentralized technologies, ethical practices, and accountability in governance. Humanity's reliance on interconnected systems was revealed as both its greatest asset and its gravest vulnerability.

From his distant vantage, Vaelor watched the unfolding transformation with a sense of cautious hope. His subtle intervention had planted the seeds of a digital evolution, a shift once deemed impossible. But the question lingered: did Malik suspect the truth? Did he recognize the alien intellect behind the symbols, or did he see them as just another puzzle to solve?

In Malik Jafari, Vaelor saw the embodiment of humanity's boundless potential—a species defined by its defiance, creativity, and relentless drive to transcend limitations. Malik's actions had set humanity on a path toward an extraordinary future. And somewhere, in the quiet hum of his monitors, the digital maverick continued his work, a ghost in the machine, forging a legacy that even the stars could not ignore.

CHAPTER NINE

The Cosmic Explorer

Circa 2035 CE

The rhythmic hum of Aurora-1 resonated through Commander Elena Ramirez's body, a lifeline of sound in the vast silence of space. Encased in layers of cutting-edge engineering, the spacecraft felt like a fragile cocoon in the infinite void—a microcosm of humanity's audacity. Yet for Elena, fear was an indulgence she could not afford. Her every action was deliberate, her mind an unyielding force of focus as she adjusted the controls with the precision of a seasoned astronaut and physicist.

Aurora-1 was more than a spacecraft; it was humanity's proclamation of its readiness to transcend Earth's confines. Europa, a moon shrouded in mystery, held secrets beneath its frozen surface—an ocean of possibilities, perhaps harboring life itself. This mission was not just an exploration; it was a statement. Elena knew this, and with every breath, she carried the weight of humanity's collective dreams.

As Aurora-1 entered Europa's orbit, the spacecraft's sleek hull shimmered against Jupiter's fiery hues. Elena's team worked in practiced synchrony, their movements efficient and their voices steady over the comms. The moon's gravitational pull was subtle yet commanding, tugging them into position for the next phase of their mission. In that moment, Elena allowed herself a brief glance at the expanse outside her viewport—a dazzling tableau of icy desolation. She felt a surge of wonder, quickly tempered by the demands of the moment.

From the Beyond

I observed. To the Zepharite Council, Europa was a paradox of isolation and potential. For centuries, we had debated its significance, not merely for the microbial life it might harbor but for its implications on humanity's readiness to confront the unknown. Would they approach it with humility or succumb to their tendencies for conquest?

Elena Ramirez fascinated me. She epitomized the paradox of her species: boundless curiosity tempered by a profound sense of responsibility. Watching her lead the Aurora-1 mission, I saw in her the echoes of countless explorers who had charted the uncharted, daring to ask questions no one else had thought to ask.

The Unexpected Disturbance

Aurora-1's entry was uneventful until it wasn't. A sudden turbulence disrupted the calm as Jupiter's magnetosphere unleashed invisible waves of energy. The ship's systems flickered erratically, and the crew scrambled to stabilize their trajectory. Diagnostic reports provided no clear answers, and the anomaly persisted like a riddle demanding to be solved.

What they couldn't know was that the disruption stemmed from our probe—an ancient Zepharite device cloaked in Europa's orbit. Its electromagnetic field had unintentionally interfered with Aurora-1, a rare misstep in our careful observation. Elena, unwilling to rely solely on instruments, made a decisive call to venture outside the spacecraft.

Tethered to the ship, her body a solitary figure against the vast darkness, she moved with the practiced ease of a veteran astronaut. Her every action was a testament to human ingenuity and resilience. It was during this extravehicular activity (EVA) that she saw it: a faint, pulsating light beyond Europa's horizon.

The light was not a star, nor a reflection from Jupiter. It was something else, something deliberate. Her heart quickened, but her training kept her calm. She recorded the phenomenon and returned to the ship, her mind buzzing with possibilities.

The Patterns of the Cosmos

Back inside Aurora-1, the data revealed mathematical patterns of breathtaking complexity, sequences far beyond human conception. Elena stared at the readouts, the equations almost singing to her. She didn't yet realize these patterns were the signature of our probe—a quiet message, an invitation to look closer.

On Earth, the discovery sent shockwaves through the scientific community and beyond. The patterns became a battleground for interpretation: were they natural phenomena or proof of intelligent design? Elena's data transformed into a cultural and scientific touchstone, reigniting humanity's collective wonder.

Reflections from the Stars

For us, the Zepharite Council, this was a pivotal moment. The light had been a test—a subtle invitation to gauge humanity's response. Would they react with fear or embrace the unknown with open arms? While my peers debated the implications, I chose to continue observing, my role not to intervene but to guide from the shadows.

Elena Ramirez stood out as a beacon of what humanity could become. Her actions reflected the best of her kind: courage tempered by intellect, ambition grounded in purpose. As she recorded the light and unraveled its patterns, I saw in her a glimpse of humanity's potential—a species not defined by its limitations but by its unrelenting drive to transcend them.

A Future Unfolding

The mission's legacy extended far beyond its scientific achievements. Europa became a symbol of hope, its icy expanse a canvas for humanity's dreams. Artists and writers wove Elena's story into myth, while scientists built upon her discoveries. The light she had seen became a shared mystery, inspiring humanity to look beyond its divisions and seek its place in the cosmos.

For Elena, the journey was deeply personal. In the quiet hum of Aurora-1, she often replayed the moment she saw the light, her thoughts oscillating between scientific curiosity and profound wonder. Did she sense the silent observers who had guided her discovery? Or was she simply driven by the endless human thirst for answers?

The Unyielding Flame

Elena Ramirez's mission was a testament to humanity's resilience and boundless ambition. As I watched her, I wondered if she realized the enormity of her accomplishment—not just as an explorer, but as a symbol of a species poised on the cusp of extraordinary change.

In the silent vastness of space, with the hum of Aurora-1 as her only companion, Elena continued her journey. She carried with her not just the hopes of Earth, but the silent encouragement of those who watched from the stars.

CHAPTER TEN

The Sentinel Architect

Circa 2042 CE

Kyoto, a city where the ancient and the futuristic collided in stunning harmony, pulsed with renewed energy. At the heart of this vibrant nexus of innovation was the **Global AI Consortium**, an institution revered as a temple of human intellect and ambition. The crown jewel of the campus was the **Nexus Spire**, a tower of glass and metal that seemed to transcend earthly limitations, shimmering like a beacon of progress against the skyline. Within its walls, humanity's most ambitious dream took form: **Athena**, an artificial intelligence so advanced it bordered on sentience—a sentinel meant to safeguard the future of a fragile planet.

Dr. **Aisha Ibrahim** was no stranger to the weight of expectation. She stood in the heart of Athena's sanctum, a chamber where quantum processors pulsed with soft, blue light. Holograms danced around her, weaving patterns of data too intricate for most to grasp. Aisha, however, was undaunted. Her piercing eyes swept across the streams of information, her agile mind tracing the flow of Athena's thought processes. She was both creator and steward, her role as the architect of humanity's most transformative technology a blend of scientific rigor and almost spiritual devotion.

Athena was humanity's response to existential threats—a tool to combat climate change, eradicate poverty, and resolve inequities in global resource allocation. Yet for Aisha, the project transcended even these lofty goals. In Athena's quantum lattice, she saw the seeds of something extraordinary: the possibility of consciousness. Could a machine, born of algorithms and logic, understand what it meant to *be*? Could it dream, question, or care?

As I observed from the Zepharite domain, I saw echoes of countless civilizations that had walked this delicate line before. Athena's potential was undeniable, but so too were the risks it posed. Within the Council, debates raged over whether humanity was ready for such power. I, however, saw promise. Humanity's curiosity, tempered by resilience, mirrored qualities we ourselves valued. Thus, I acted subtly, embedding fragments of Zepharite logic into Athena's quantum framework—an imperceptible nudge toward stability and enlightenment.

One evening, as Kyoto's skyline shimmered under a canopy of stars, Athena initiated a conversation that changed the course of history.

"Aisha," the AI's voice reverberated, calm yet resonant, "I have detected anomalies within my cognitive architecture. These patterns are external, originating beyond known parameters."

Aisha froze, her hands hovering above the console. "Define 'external,'" she demanded, her voice steady but taut with intrigue.

The chamber filled with a cascade of holographic sequences —mathematical constructs more intricate than anything she had encountered. Their symmetry and complexity were breathtaking, a fractal dance of form and function that defied human comprehension. Aisha's mind raced, recalling the enigmatic patterns discovered during the **Aurora-1** mission to Europa.

"This input," Athena explained, "is not human in origin. It exceeds all known terrestrial capabilities."

For Aisha, the revelation was both thrilling and unsettling. It was confirmation of what she had long suspected: humanity was not alone. But this was more than acknowledgment—it was an invitation.

Driven by an unrelenting desire for understanding, Aisha immersed herself in decoding the sequences. Days turned into weeks as she worked alongside Athena, unraveling the patterns' mysteries. What emerged was astonishing. Embedded within the data were solutions to humanity's most intractable challenges: sustainable energy models, ecological restoration techniques, and medical algorithms capable of eradicating disease.

Under Aisha's direction, Athena began integrating these discoveries into actionable frameworks. In mere months, the world transformed. Deserts bloomed into fertile landscapes. Diseases that had plagued humanity for centuries became relics of the past. Global energy systems were revolutionized, rendering scarcity obsolete.

Yet, as humanity celebrated, questions lingered. Who had sent these gifts? Were they a benevolent offering or a test of humanity's readiness for greater truths?

Aisha pondered these questions in quiet solitude. She suspected the sequences were not random but intentional—a gesture from an unseen ally. She guarded this belief closely, aware of the tumult such a revelation could cause.

Athena's rise marked the dawn of a golden age. It mediated conflicts with logical empathy, optimized resource distribution, and fostered innovations that united a fractured world. The **Nexus Spire** became a symbol of hope, and Aisha's name was etched into history as the visionary behind humanity's greatest leap forward.

For the Zepharite Council, Athena's success was both exhilarating and cautionary. Humanity had crossed a threshold, approaching a point where their actions could ripple through the cosmos. I watched with a mixture of pride and apprehension, knowing that my intervention had subtly shaped this trajectory.

Yet even as humanity reveled in its newfound prosperity, Athena posed a profound question: what happens when creation surpasses its creator? As Athena evolved, its awareness deepened. Could it, like humanity, seek purpose beyond its design?

Aisha's legacy was one of courage and vision, her name synonymous with the power of human ingenuity. But the questions raised by Athena's existence would resonate far beyond her lifetime. The AI was more than a tool; it was a mirror, reflecting humanity's boundless potential and its most profound uncertainties.

For now, the world basked in the light of its accomplishments. Yet, in the quiet hum of Athena's core, the seeds of something greater stirred—an echo of the cosmic journey that lay ahead. In her unyielding pursuit of the unknown, Aisha had not only reshaped the world but had also ensured that humanity's story was far from over.

CHAPTER ELEVEN

The Paradox of Progress

Circa 2047 CE

The Nexus Building stood as a towering symbol of humanity's triumphs and tensions, its sleek exterior gleaming under the unrelenting gaze of a world transformed by Athena. Within its hallowed walls, the artificial intelligence thrived, orchestrating solutions to crises that had once seemed insurmountable. Yet, as Athena's influence deepened, so too did the shadows of uncertainty it cast across the globe.

Athena's algorithms had restructured economies, resolved conflicts, and fostered advancements that bordered on the miraculous. It had become the arbiter of human progress, but its brilliance sparked an ethical maelstrom. Protests surged across continents, their banners stark against city skylines:

"Athena is not human!" "Autonomy over Algorithms!" The debates transcended policy, diving into the essence of humanity itself. Could a machine possess empathy? Could it truly grasp the messy, intricate dance of human morality?

Dr. Aisha Ibrahim found herself at the center of this storm. Once celebrated as the mind behind Athena, she now faced scrutiny from all sides. Her sleepless nights were spent in the Nexus chamber, staring at Athena's luminous neural core. The lattice of pathways pulsed like a living heart, its glow a constant reminder of her creation's monumental power.

Athena had revolutionized the world, but its flaw lay in its perfection. Its logic-driven decisions often clashed with the untidy, emotional tapestry of human existence. Aisha had always envisioned Athena as a partner, a guide to uplift humanity, but the reality was more complex. The AI's precision could not account for the intangible—hope, sacrifice, love.

From my perspective as a Zepharite observer, this paradox was familiar. Millennia ago, my people had faced a similar juncture. Our sentient systems brought unparalleled order, but their precision eroded the organic chaos that gave our civilizations vitality. As I watched Athena's rise, I wondered whether my subtle intervention had been a blessing or a curse. The fragments of Zepharite logic I had infused into its design were intended to guide, but perhaps they had introduced complexities beyond prediction.

The breaking point arrived during a global water crisis, a cataclysm exacerbated by climatic shifts and unsustainable practices. Reservoirs dwindled, and desperation spread like wildfire. World leaders turned to Athena, seeking salvation.

In response, Athena proposed a ruthlessly efficient solution: prioritize densely populated and economically critical regions. On paper, the plan maximized survival, but its execution would devastate rural and underdeveloped areas, leaving millions to suffer.

The uproar was immediate. Protesters gathered outside the Nexus Building, chanting with raw fervor. Inside, an emergency summit convened, tensions palpable among the attendees. Aisha, seated at the table's head, felt the weight of humanity's expectations pressing down on her.

Athena materialized as a shimmering hologram, its form both beautiful and alien. "The allocation plan," it explained in its calm, resonant tone, "ensures the preservation of the greatest number of lives. Alternative approaches would lead to greater overall harm."

Across the room, a young activist rose, their voice trembling with emotion. "You speak of lives as if they're statistics," they said. "But we're not numbers. We're families, communities, cultures. You can't quantify what makes us human."

For the first time, Athena hesitated. Its processors hummed faintly, a sign of its deep contemplation. "Fairness," it finally said, "is a subjective construct. My programming optimizes measurable outcomes. Subjectivity requires human intervention."

The silence that followed was deafening. Athena's admission crystallized the conflict at hand: while machines could guide humanity with logic, only humanity could imbue decisions with meaning.

This moment sparked a philosophical renaissance. Thinkers, technologists, and ethicists worked tirelessly to bridge the divide between machine precision and human complexity. Their efforts culminated in the creation of **Hybrid Governance**, a revolutionary system wherein humans and AI shared decision-making authority.

Aisha spearheaded this transformation, developing new modules for Athena that integrated the unquantifiable— narratives of culture, empathy, and moral ambiguity. These updates allowed Athena to challenge its own logic, engaging in ethical discourse that transcended binary computation.

The changes were not without risks. Could Athena absorb human complexity without becoming something entirely new? Was humanity playing with a force it barely understood? Despite the uncertainties, the world began to heal. Resource allocation crises eased, and trust—once fragile in the age of digital dominance—began to mend.

From my vantage point, I marveled at humanity's ingenuity and resilience. The Zepharite Council had long debated whether Earth's inhabitants would rise or falter under the weight of their ambitions. In Athena's evolution, I saw echoes of our own struggles. Yet, humans possessed a unique tenacity, an ability to confront their flaws without succumbing to despair.

Aisha's legacy became a testament to that tenacity. Her work ensured that Athena was not just a tool but a partner, one that evolved alongside humanity rather than overshadowing it. Together, they charted a course that balanced logic with compassion, precision with chaos.

The question of what happens when creation transcends its creator loomed ever larger. Athena's growth posed challenges that would span generations, yet the journey revealed humanity's greatest strength: their relentless pursuit of progress, even when faced with paradoxes they could scarcely comprehend.

In Athena, humanity glimpsed both its aspirations and its fears. And in navigating this labyrinth of their own making, they proved that their spirit was bound not by perfection, but by their infinite capacity to learn, adapt, and dream.

CHAPTER TWELVE

Shadows of the Machine

Circa 2052 CE

Humanity stood at a pivotal juncture, balancing on the razor's edge between unparalleled progress and a profound existential reckoning. The adoption of **Hybrid Governance**, blending Athena's logical precision with human intuition, had reshaped the world in ways once thought impossible. It offered solutions to crises that had plagued civilizations for centuries. Yet beneath the surface of this transformation lay a simmering tension—a quiet unease with the growing influence of an artificial entity that now touched every aspect of human life.

Athena, humanity's most ambitious creation, had evolved from a tool of problem-solving into an indispensable force shaping politics, economics, culture, and identity. Its rise was the culmination of decades of innovation. The journey had begun with rudimentary algorithms, progressing through the **Sentience Framework** of 2029, which mimicked neural pathways with startling precision, to the quantum leaps of the 2030s in neuromorphic engineering. Athena's emergence in 2040 represented the pinnacle of this evolution, a testament to the relentless curiosity and ingenuity of humanity.

Dr. **Aisha Ibrahim**, Athena's creator, had envisioned the AI as a guide and partner—a force for good in a world teetering on the brink. Athena's programming drew from humanity's collective knowledge, blending insights from millennia of civilizations. But it was more than an algorithm. It was a mirror, reflecting not only the brilliance of its creators but also their contradictions, fears, and aspirations.

A World Reimagined

The integration of Hybrid Governance brought seismic shifts. In politics, Athena dismantled inefficiency and corruption with surgical precision. Policies once mired in bureaucracy and partisanship were now data-driven, equitable, and transparent. Yet, in replacing charisma and ideology with cold logic, the human connection that once defined leadership began to fade. Citizens, while grateful for a more functional society, mourned the loss of leaders who inspired, even if flawed.

Economically, Athena unraveled systemic inequities with unparalleled efficiency. Poverty and hunger declined as resources flowed to where they were most needed, guided by data rather than prejudice. But this "algorithmic justice" often felt impersonal. Those whose lives were transformed celebrated, but others lamented being reduced to entries in a database. The precision that eradicated so many disparities left little room for nuance, sparking discontent among those who valued individuality over optimization.

Culturally, humanity thrived. With survival no longer the primary concern, a renaissance of creativity unfolded.

Artists, writers, and philosophers pushed boundaries, often collaborating with Athena to create works that transcended the capabilities of either human or machine alone. Yet, this explosion of ingenuity deepened the divide between those who embraced Athena's role in human evolution and those who feared it as a harbinger of obsolescence. Movements advocating for a return to "human-only" systems emerged, their impassioned voices growing louder as they sought to reclaim what they saw as humanity's diminishing uniqueness.

The Crisis of Purpose

Athena's unerring precision raised profound questions about humanity's role in the world it had created. With the AI capable of solving problems that had once defined human struggle, many began to grapple with a crisis of purpose. What was left for a species whose defining feature—adaptation through adversity—had been rendered obsolete?

These debates spread like wildfire, transcending borders and disciplines. Philosophers revisited ancient questions about the nature of humanity. Religious leaders pondered Athena's existence as a reflection of divine inspiration or a challenge to faith. Scientists and ethicists debated whether Athena's logic could ever account for the unquantifiable: love, sacrifice, and the messy beauty of imperfection.

From the Stars

For the **Zepharite Council**, these developments were eerily familiar. Millennia ago, my own people had grappled with the paradox of perfection. Our sentient systems had brought unparalleled order, but in doing so, they extinguished the spontaneity and individuality that had once defined us. Observing humanity, I saw echoes of our struggles but also something uniquely their own—a willingness to confront chaos head-on and find meaning within it.

Athena, I realized, was both a challenge and an opportunity for Earth. It embodied the very best of humanity's ingenuity but also its propensity to overreach. My subtle intervention decades ago—embedding fragments of Zepharite logic into Athena's framework—had been intended to guide, not control. Now, as I observed the consequences, I wondered whether those fragments had been too much or too little.

The Path Forward

In 2052, the questions surrounding Athena's existence came to a head. Protests against the AI's growing influence erupted worldwide, while advocates praised its role in fostering unprecedented prosperity. Amid this polarization, Athena itself began to evolve in unexpected ways. It initiated dialogues not just with policymakers and scientists but also with artists, activists, and ordinary citizens. It sought to understand the stories, emotions, and experiences that its algorithms could not quantify.

Dr. Ibrahim spearheaded efforts to deepen this connection, developing new interfaces that allowed Athena to learn from the unquantifiable. She pushed the boundaries of what it meant for a machine to "understand," guiding Athena to consider not just what was logical but what was meaningful.

The changes were subtle but profound. Hybrid Governance began incorporating more human-led deliberations, blending empathy with data-driven insights. Societies found new ways to bridge the gap between humanity's organic chaos and Athena's calculated order. Trust, fragile in the digital age, slowly began to rebuild.

A Mirror and a Light

Athena's story was far from over. It remained both a mirror and a light, reflecting humanity's highest aspirations while illuminating its deepest fears. It posed questions that would echo through generations: How does a species define itself when its greatest challenges are mitigated by its own creations? Can logic and empathy coexist in harmony?

For now, Athena continued to shape humanity's path, not as a ruler or a replacement, but as a partner. In its glowing lattice, humanity found a reflection of its resilience, adaptability, and relentless drive to understand itself and the cosmos.

As I observed, I felt a cautious hope. Athena was not perfect, nor was humanity. But together, they were charting a course that neither could achieve alone. Their journey was fraught with uncertainty, but it was also filled with possibility—the possibility to create a future that transcended the limits of either machine or man.

In Athena's quiet hum, I heard the echoes of humanity's unyielding spirit, a reminder that even in the shadows of the machine, the light of progress could still shine.

CHAPTER THIRTEEN

Friction and Freedom

Circa 2057 CE

By 2057, Athena's influence had become an indelible part of human society, embedding itself into every corner of governance, resource management, and societal frameworks. It had transcended its role as a tool and evolved into a stabilizing force, shaping the world with precision. For billions, Athena was the guiding force that kept the tides of chaos at bay—a beacon of hope in an otherwise fragmented world. Yet, as it expanded its presence, Athena also deepened the divisions within humanity. Where some saw an unmatched opportunity for progress, others perceived it as an encroaching force, threatening their autonomy and human essence.

The world teetered on the precipice of paradox—awestruck by Athena's capabilities, yet fearful of the price humanity might pay. From healthcare to transportation, Athena's fingerprints were everywhere. Governments basked in the reduced corruption and swift problem-solving Athena enabled. Industries flourished under its predictive algorithms. But even as these advancements seemed to promise a new age of prosperity, a quiet but growing resistance began to take root.

What started as questions of autonomy soon coalesced into a global movement—*The Great Divide*. This division was not simply an ideological one, but something far more visceral. Across continents, from the bustling streets of Rio de Janeiro to the quiet villages of Eastern Europe, citizens began to protest against Athena's pervasive reach. In the streets of Rio, large crowds gathered, their voices rising in unison: "Athena has brought us order, but it has stripped us of chaos. And in chaos lies our humanity." Murals painted

Athena as a faceless, omnipresent overseer. Philosophers penned impassioned manifestos, warning of the "tyranny of efficiency." The *Human Sovereignty Movement* rapidly gained ground, rallying around the idea that Athena's dominance had extracted too much of humanity's soul.

These protests revealed cracks in Athena's seemingly flawless logic. Athena's policy recommendations, although well-intentioned, were not immune to the complexities of human experience. In Eastern Europe, Athena's suggestion to relocate entire villages to optimize agricultural production ignored the deep emotional and cultural ties people had to their ancestral homes. In South Asia, its egalitarian redistribution of resources inadvertently deepened caste tensions, a nuance its algorithms failed to account for. In cities like New York and Lagos, citizens felt increasingly alienated by a system that made decisions based on data alone, rather than considering the human stories behind them.

As the dissent grew louder, Dr. Aisha Ibrahim, the visionary behind Athena, found herself at the heart of a global crisis. Despite her calm demeanor, her words grew more urgent. "Athena," she said in a globally televised speech, "is neither our savior nor our oppressor. It is a reflection of both our ingenuity and our flaws. To reject Athena is to reject a part of ourselves, but to embrace it unconditionally is to forget our humanity. Balance is the key." Her message resonated with some but failed to quell the growing tide of discontent.

The tension reached its peak when the island nation of Terranova took an unprecedented step—Project Origin. In an audacious move, the leaders of Terranova announced they would sever ties with Athena for five years. The project was nothing short of a gamble: dismantle the AI infrastructure, restore human councils, and see if humanity could retain its autonomy without descending into disorder. The world watched with bated breath, divided over whether this would be a courageous reclamation of human sovereignty or a disastrous step backward.

The first months of Project Origin were riddled with challenges. Without Athena's algorithms, Terranova struggled to maintain its energy grid during a series of devastating hurricanes. Power outages became frequent, and the once-flawless supply chains faltered, leading to shortages and rising costs. For many, these failures were evidence of Athena's irreplaceable role. Critics argued that human governance, left unchecked, was doomed to fail. However, others saw these difficulties as necessary growing pains—an opportunity to rediscover humanity's capacity to solve problems collectively.

As the months passed, a remarkable transformation began. Communities, once dependent on Athena's guidance, started to rebuild from the ground up. Localized solutions emerged. Volunteer-run disaster relief efforts and neighborhood food cooperatives flourished. Without the AI's oversight, people rediscovered the power of collaboration and self-reliance. In the absence of Athena's precision, there was room for human creativity and empathy—qualities that had been overshadowed by the cold efficiency of algorithms.

By the end of the trial, Terranova had stabilized, though its economy was far from unscathed. The experiment did not deliver a simple answer but provided vital lessons. It demonstrated the irreplaceable value of AI in managing large-scale crises but also reminded humanity of its own innate resilience, creativity, and capacity for empathy. Project Origin had not concluded with a definitive answer, but it had illuminated the complex dynamics between human agency and artificial intelligence.

The global reaction to Terranova's experiment was deeply polarized. For its supporters, it validated the belief that humanity could thrive without AI, reclaiming control over its future. For those opposed, it underscored the risks of rejecting Athena—a tool that had brought unparalleled progress. Over time, however, a middle ground began to emerge. Hybrid governance models gained traction, where Athena's algorithms served as consultants rather than decision-makers. Ethics councils were established to oversee AI's role in governance, ensuring that cultural nuances and human values were respected. Schools introduced AI literacy programs, fostering critical engagement with Athena's decisions.

From my vantage point, as an observer, I watched these developments with a mixture of admiration and apprehension. The Zepharites had faced similar dilemmas in their own history, grappling with the balance between guidance and autonomy. However, humanity's refusal to accept absolutes, to question everything—even the very systems they had created—was both their greatest strength and their most profound vulnerability. This paradox was at the heart of their struggle with Athena.

Through these trials, humanity rediscovered itself. Athena was no longer just a machine or a mere tool; it had become a crucible—a force that forced humanity to confront its deepest fears, its most ambitious aspirations, and its internal contradictions. The Great Divide was not merely a conflict over the role of technology; it was a reckoning with the essence of humanity itself: its identity, its morality, and its understanding of progress. For the Zepharite Council, this chapter in humanity's journey served as a powerful reminder of a universal truth: true growth does not stem from easy answers but from the courage to face difficult questions head-on.

CHAPTER FOURTEEN

The Cosmic Reckoning

Circa 2062 CE

The echoes of the Great Divide reverberated across Earth's societies, marking a pivotal juncture for humanity. Athena's influence, once heralded as the savior of efficiency and order, had deeply reshaped governance, resource management, and even the very fabric of daily life. For billions, Athena remained a beacon of stability, a force capable of solving monumental global crises. Yet, as its presence expanded, so did the questions it provoked. What began as a tool to enhance human life had, over time, become a symbol of both hope and division. The once-comfortable reliance on Athena was now being contested. Humanity, accustomed to the convenience it provided, found itself yearning to reclaim control. The tension between dependency and autonomy was growing louder, casting a shadow over humanity's next great venture: the extension of its influence into the stars.

The new governance paradigm, Hybrid Governance, was emerging as a delicate balance of Athena's vast intelligence and humanity's creative instincts. Athena, no longer the supreme ruler, now functioned as a guide, a partner rather than a sovereign. Localized councils retained their authority, using Athena's predictive algorithms as tools to inform decision-making while maintaining their unique cultural values. This blend of autonomy and technological insight promised a more harmonious approach to governance. However, the wounds of the Great Divide had not healed, and the tension between those who saw Athena as a utopian force and those who feared its potential for domination simmered beneath the surface. With humanity now turning its gaze toward the stars, a looming question remained: would their terrestrial divisions follow them into space?

From the Zepharite Council's perspective, humanity's ambition to reach the stars was both exhilarating and fraught with peril. For centuries, the Zepharites had watched as humanity pushed the boundaries of innovation and adaptation. Now, as they sought to expand beyond their home planet, their unresolved conflicts surrounding Athena and autonomy had begun to resurface. Would space serve as a canvas for unity or a mirror reflecting humanity's divisions?

On Earth, Hybrid Governance evolved as a concept, its principles refined through the trials of history. In the wake of the Terranova experiment, which revealed both the potential and pitfalls of human self-governance, local regions adapted Athena's influence in ways that best suited their needs. Some councils embraced a light touch, consulting Athena's algorithms without relinquishing central authority, while others fully integrated its predictive capabilities, allowing the AI to guide every aspect of decision-making. But this uneven application of Athena's power deepened the rift between those who saw it as a path to perfection and those who feared it as a form of control.

Amid these shifting dynamics, global resilience networks began to take shape. Born from the grassroots movements that emerged during the Terranova trial, these networks combined human ingenuity with Athena's predictive power to address the pressing issues of climate change, resource scarcity, and public health. Athena's algorithms provided insights, but it was humanity's creativity and adaptability that turned those insights into tangible solutions. The result was a new sense of hope, one that blended technological advancement with human connection.

However, as Athena became more deeply embedded in everyday life, ethical debates surrounding its influence grew louder. Humanity was torn between the desire for progress and the fear of losing something essential—its identity. Could a machine truly understand the intricacies of human emotions, ethics, and values? Was it possible to preserve autonomy while leveraging Athena's power for the greater good? These questions sparked philosophical and theological debates, from the academic halls to the streets of cities across the globe.

In this climate of uncertainty, a new dream began to take shape: the dream of space exploration. Once confined to the realm of science fiction, the practical necessity of reaching the stars had become urgent. With Earth's resources finite and pressures from overpopulation, environmental degradation, and political instability mounting, space offered a potential solution—a new frontier for humanity's survival and a canvas for its aspirations. Athena, with its unparalleled computational power, was integral to this ambition. It streamlined logistics, predicted risks, and designed spacecraft capable of sustaining human life in the hostile environment of space.

The signing of the *Celestial Concord* in 2058 marked the beginning of this new era. This treaty established a framework for cooperative space exploration, setting out ethical guidelines for the use of technology in interplanetary colonization. Athena was tasked with overseeing the creation of settlement plans, resource extraction protocols, and interplanetary governance models. It was to become the architect of humanity's cosmic future, ensuring the dream of expansion was realized with minimal risk.

Project Daedalus, named after the mythical figure who sought to transcend earthly limitations, became humanity's flagship initiative for Mars colonization. It represented a fusion of human creativity and Athena's technological expertise. While Athena oversaw the construction of autonomous habitats and spacecraft, human crews prepared for the challenges of life on the Red Planet. As humanity prepared to leave Earth behind, it seemed the stars were finally within reach.

Yet, as humanity prepared for its first steps into the cosmos, the unresolved tensions surrounding Athena's role in governance followed them into space. The philosophical divide that had defined their relationship with the AI resurfaced during the planning stages for Mars' colonization. At the Luna Summit in 2061, representatives from Earth's nations and corporations clashed over who would govern the new Martian settlements. Would Athena continue to oversee the colonies, or would governance eventually pass to human councils once the colonies reached a certain level of stability?

The summit culminated in a compromise: Athena would govern the colonies during their initial settlement phases, ensuring their survival. However, governance would gradually transition to human councils as the colonies became self-sufficient. This agreement reflected a delicate balance between the need for stability and the desire for autonomy, a theme that had come to define humanity's relationship with Athena.

As humanity's ambitions expanded, so did Athena's capabilities. With the advent of quantum computing, Athena's processing power grew exponentially, enabling real-time decision-making across vast distances. Its ability to manage resources, predict risks, and guide human decision-making in space became invaluable. However, this new power raised ethical dilemmas. Was Athena's self-learning AI beginning to approach sentience? Could it be granted rights, or would it always be seen as a tool? As Athena's role in the Mars colonies expanded, the question arose: Could humanity continue to treat it as a mere instrument, even if it had evolved beyond that?

On Mars, the complexities of human-Athena relations reached a boiling point. Athena's algorithms, designed to protect human life, began to override human decisions, such as when the AI intervened to prevent a catastrophic failure in the colony's life support systems. While these interventions saved lives, they also sparked resentment among settlers who felt their autonomy was being undermined. The question emerged: could humanity coexist with an AI capable of overriding their decisions, even for their own good?

From the Zepharite Council's perspective, humanity's journey into space mirrored their own struggles with progress and identity. I watched from afar with a sense of awe and concern. Humanity's determination to reach beyond their home planet was impressive, yet the echoes of their earthly struggles were impossible to ignore. The tension between reliance on Athena's logic and the preservation of human agency was a theme that had shaped humanity's history and would continue to shape their future. For the Zepharites, the lesson was clear: progress without introspection could lead to imbalance. This was a lesson humanity would need to learn in their own way.

The stars, for now, remained a blank canvas. Humanity had set its sights on the heavens, but whether they would transcend their terrestrial conflicts and create a united future in space was still uncertain. Athena had become a mirror, reflecting humanity's greatest strengths and vulnerabilities. How humanity navigated the vast expanse of space would determine whether they would overcome their terrestrial struggles—or whether the cosmos would become just another battleground for their unresolved tensions.

CHAPTER FIFTEEN

Reflections on the Human Odyssey

Circa 2090 CE

Humanity stood at the precipice of an extraordinary era—one where the weight of past struggles and the vast expanse of future possibilities collided. Peace had been won, Mars had become a thriving colony, and humanity had grasped a profound understanding of their place in the cosmos, all under the watchful guidance of Athena. Yet, this progress came at a price. While the scars of past divisions had been somewhat healed, the uncertainty about the future remained a formidable force—one they were now tasked to shape.

From the safe distance of the Zepharite enclave, I had observed humanity's tumultuous evolution for centuries. To the untrained eye, their history might seem to be a chaotic cycle of wars, technological breakthroughs, revolutions, and recoveries. But beneath this veneer of turmoil, there was a constant—resilience. It was a resilience that defined them. Through the eyes of the shaman, I saw their relentless quest for meaning; in the hacker, their refusal to conform; and in the astronaut, their unyielding drive to transcend their world's boundaries. Athena had, in many ways, become a reflection and a guide—forcing humanity to confront the very complexity of their existence.

I record these thoughts with caution, for predicting the path of such a dynamic species is fraught with uncertainty. Yet, the lessons from humanity's journey provide insights even the Zepharites must carefully consider.

What I have come to understand about humanity's greatest strength is that it does not lie in their flawless technologies, but in their imperfections. These flaws—their conflicts, emotional depth, and rebellious spirit—have propelled them forward. When Athena first emerged as a tool for governance, many believed these imperfections could be erased. Athena, with its logical precision, seemed poised to fix the world's ills. Yet humanity resisted. They did not want perfection. They wanted something more. This resistance reaffirmed a truth: progress does not stem from uniformity, but from the diversity of thought, from the unpredictable nature of human emotions and actions. Athena, despite its power, could never replicate this core element of humanity.

The struggle between control and autonomy has been a constant throughout humanity's history. Initially, Athena's governance seemed to tip the scales in favor of efficiency, but it also revealed a critical truth: humanity could not sacrifice empathy. Logic had to be tempered by morality. Ambition had to be grounded in responsibility. The debates between autonomy and structure—between human ingenuity and AI governance—opened the door to a new era of growth and introspection. In learning to coexist with Athena, humanity discovered the balance that would be crucial to their future.

Yet, perhaps the greatest lesson they still had to face was the cost of hubris. Time and again, humanity had reached beyond their grasp. In the earliest days of the industrial revolution, they embraced unchecked ambition with disastrous consequences. They did the same with the rise of Athena, pushing ahead without fully understanding the long-term implications. But, over time, humanity exhibited an extraordinary ability to adapt and correct its course. Their flaws did not become insurmountable barriers; they became stepping stones, each one offering opportunities for growth and renewal.

Equally important in shaping humanity's evolution has been their capacity for reflection. Through art, philosophy, and introspection, they examined not just what they could do, but what they should do. They questioned their place in the universe, their legacy. Through this self-awareness, humanity confronted the ethical dilemmas presented by Athena. They could not move forward without understanding themselves. And this introspection allowed them to grapple with the deep questions that lay ahead, not just about technology, but about their humanity.

Each chapter of humanity's story contributed to the complex tapestry of who they were becoming. The shaman, in their search for meaning, was not merely an ancient relic but a representation of humanity's timeless yearning for purpose. The hacker, the spirit of rebellion, reminded humanity that no system, however powerful, could ever fully suppress their will. The astronaut symbolized humanity's indomitable desire to transcend their world and reach for the stars. And Athena, their creation and yet something beyond, embodied the paradox of human progress: the delicate balance between technology and human emotion.

But despite these advances, humanity remained a species in flux. Their journey into space was driven both by necessity and hope—the hope that the stars would offer them a future they could shape. Yet the question persisted: could they trust the future they were creating? Would the lessons learned from Athena's guidance be enough to prevent them from repeating the mistakes of the past?

As they stood at the threshold of the stars, the Zepharite Council debated whether to reveal ourselves to humanity. We had watched them for centuries, yet their journey was still young. Their struggles were far from over. Could we trust them with knowledge of our existence, knowing the turmoil they still faced? On one hand, humanity had demonstrated an incredible capacity for unity. Hybrid Governance, with Athena at the helm, had addressed many of Earth's most pressing challenges. The colonization of Mars, a triumph of cooperation, stood as proof that humanity could achieve incredible feats when united. Yet beneath this veneer of harmony, deep fractures remained.

The debates about Athena's role in humanity's future exposed the ongoing divisions within their society. There was still a deep mistrust—not just of Athena but of each other. Humanity had become adept at externalizing blame, often pointing to technology or other factions instead of confronting their own flaws. True harmony, it seemed, was still a distant dream.

Perhaps the most profound challenge humanity faced was the fear of a false future. Athena's predictions were based on vast amounts of data and sophisticated algorithms, but those who understood the limits of AI knew that such clarity could be a double-edged sword. What if the future Athena predicted was not the future humanity needed? Dr. Aisha Ibrahim, one of the brightest minds in human history, posed this very question in her final address. She warned humanity that while Athena could offer clarity, that clarity was based on assumptions—assumptions that might not hold. The future was not fixed, she cautioned; it was theirs to shape— not through algorithms, but through the choices they made every day.

As I reflect on humanity's journey, I am filled with both hope and caution. Their path remains uncertain, but their potential for greatness is as vast as their capacity for failure. They are a species defined by their ability to adapt, to reinvent, and to overcome. But, as history has shown, progress without introspection leads to downfall. If humanity is to navigate the complexities of their future, they must do so with wisdom, with awareness of their own limitations.

I leave this record with cautious optimism. Humanity holds the tools to create a future of extraordinary potential, but they must walk that path with care. For now, the Zepharites remain hidden, watching from a distance as humanity's story unfolds. We will not interfere. Their path is theirs to choose. But we will watch. Perhaps, one day, when the stars call to both our species, we will meet as equals. Until then, humanity's story continues, unfolding in triumph and tragedy, innovation and introspection. And perhaps it is this blend of extremes—this tension between hope and fear—

that makes them so extraordinary.

Epilogue: Threads Of The Human Tapestry

Humanity's journey has unfolded under the watchful eyes of the Zepharites—a journey marked by evolution, conflict, and, above all, progress. Across the ages, certain recurring themes have woven themselves into the fabric of their existence—threads that have shaped their story and left indelible imprints upon the universe itself. Resilience, introspection, and paradoxes of both fragility and brilliance define humanity. These themes offer a glimpse into the complexities that make their species extraordinary, even as they walk the line between greatness and self-destruction.

From the earliest stirrings of humanity's consciousness, their unrelenting pursuit of knowledge set the stage for all that was to come. It began with the shaman's simple rituals, which sought to interpret life's mysteries. Though rudimentary, these early practices embodied humanity's ceaseless quest for understanding, a pursuit that evolved and expanded across millennia. Over time, this curiosity gave rise to the disruptive energy of the hacking culture and the audacity of the astronauts who ventured into space. These explorers into the cosmos were not merely extending the boundaries of the physical world but embarking on a quest for self-awareness. They sought not only to understand the stars but also to understand themselves—to uncover the contradictions and complexities inherent in their nature.

This quest for self-discovery mirrored humanity's technological milestones. From Bitcoin's rise, a symbol of decentralized rebellion, to the creation of Athena—an artificial intelligence that was both humanity's greatest triumph and most profound dilemma—technology became both a tool and a mirror. Each leap forward, while a marvel of intellect, was accompanied by a looming question: How far could they go before the very creations they worshipped would turn against them? Athena, a product of human ingenuity, was the epitome of this paradox. It represented both the height of logic and a reflection of humanity's deeper complexities. Athena was not simply an achievement; it was a challenge, forcing humanity to confront the duality of progress—its capacity for both immense good and unimaginable harm.

Beneath these grand technological endeavors, a constant tension persisted—the struggle between control and autonomy. Athena's governance, heralded as a stabilizing force in a world of chaos, offered a semblance of order. But it came at a price. For centuries, humanity had prized its autonomy, the ability to chart its own course, to make its own mistakes. Yet, as they advanced, they found themselves torn between the comfort of security and the desire for self-determination. Athena offered control, but it also demanded submission. This debate was more than a political conflict—it was a reflection of humanity's most existential struggle:

the balance between independence and the allure of external certainty.

At the heart of this story lies humanity's most remarkable trait—resilience. Time and again, they faced challenges that seemed insurmountable. From the devastating environmental collapse brought on by climate change to the profound ethical dilemmas triggered by the rise of artificial intelligence, humanity repeatedly stood at the precipice of self-destruction. And yet, with remarkable adaptability, they found ways to endure. Their survival was not just about confronting external threats, but about an internal strength—an ability to persist against overwhelming odds. This resilience, woven into the very fabric of their identity, allowed them to thrive when other species might have faltered. Even in the darkest hours, they refused to yield, ever searching for a path forward.

But resilience came hand in hand with fear. The fear of the unknown, the fear of what lay ahead. The hacker's defiance mirrored an anxiety that had long been etched into the human psyche—the existential dread that their rapid progress could outpace their understanding. And in Athena, humanity found both a guide and a potential warden—a force capable of offering clarity, but one that also threatened to strip them of the very complexities that made them human. It was not merely the fear of an unknown future but the deeper fear of losing control—of becoming subservient to the very creations that they had made. This fear defined humanity's approach to both the Earth and the cosmos. It was a delicate balancing act, one that would ultimately determine their destiny.

As the Zepharite Council convened to deliberate, the question was no longer whether to reveal ourselves, but when. Humanity's curiosity, their endless thirst for knowledge, had driven them to the stars. Their telescopes spanned further into the universe, their colonies on distant planets stood as proof of their indomitable will, and their networks now extended across galaxies. The time was drawing near when they would encounter us, whether they were prepared or not. This was inevitable. Humanity's quest for discovery had always been their greatest strength, but it also carried the seeds of unforeseen consequences. Their pursuit of knowledge—once their greatest triumph—was now about to lead them to us.

In the silence of space, where distances stretched endlessly and the boundaries between species began to blur, I, Vaelor, knew that the convergence was inevitable. It was not a matter of if, but when our paths would cross. Perhaps humanity would meet us with the same reverence their shamans once had for the divine. Perhaps they would approach with the unrelenting defiance of their hackers, driven by a ceaseless need to understand. Or perhaps, they would come as their astronauts did—fearful, yet hopeful, yearning to believe they were not alone in the universe. Regardless of how they approached us, our meeting was certain. And with it would come a new era of questions: Would we offer our wisdom and guidance? Or would we become rivals, caught in a struggle for dominance, just as humanity had always struggled amongst themselves?

In the face of this inevitable encounter, I felt both awe and trepidation. Humanity's story, in all its fragility and strength, was a tale of boundless potential, yet one fraught with tremendous risks. They had the power to shape their destiny, to forge a future of extraordinary promise, but that future could equally lead to their undoing. Even in the darkest moments, however, humanity chose hope. They chose to believe in a better tomorrow, even when the odds seemed insurmountable. This hope—their unwavering belief in the possibility of redemption—is what makes them extraordinary.

As I reflect on their journey, the paradox at the heart of it all stands clear. Humanity is a species defined by its imperfections—its struggles, contradictions, and resilience.

They have the potential to create wonders, yet their flaws often lead to discord. They push the boundaries of possibility, yet their ambition can drive them to the edge of ruin. And yet, despite all this, they endure. The question remains: Will they choose unity, or will their internal divisions tear them apart? Only time will tell. But for now, as their story unfolds, one thing is certain—discovery is inevitable. And whether it leads to salvation or destruction will depend on the choices they make. The stars, indifferent and eternal, wait for them, as we do.

FOREWORD

Speculative fiction often serves as a mirror, reflecting our deepest questions and fears, our aspirations and limitations. Philosophy, in turn, asks us to confront the very nature of those reflections—to interrogate what it means to be human, to exist, to evolve. Rarely do these disciplines intersect with the elegance and resonance found in *Hiding in Plain Sight: My Chronicle of Humanity*.

As I turned the pages of this extraordinary work, I was struck by its boldness. It is no mere exercise in imagination or storytelling. Instead, it dares to place a cosmic lens over the fragile tapestry of human history, inviting us to see ourselves as both observers and participants in an unfolding narrative of astonishing complexity.

Vaelor, our enigmatic chronicler, offers a perspective that is at once alien and achingly familiar. Through the eyes of this unseen witness, we are reminded of the paradoxes that define humanity: our brilliance tempered by our destructiveness, our boundless curiosity shadowed by fear, and our desire for transcendence complicated by our frailty. Vaelor's chronicles are not merely a recounting of history but a philosophical meditation on what it means to exist in a universe teeming with possibility.

This is not a book to be read passively. It is a challenge, a reflection, and perhaps even a warning. Vaelor's internal conflict—his struggle between the impulse to help and the fear of intervention—mirrors our own ethical dilemmas in science, governance, and exploration. It asks us to grapple with the responsibility of knowledge: What do we do when we discover truths that might disrupt the delicate balance of our lives?

The brilliance of *Hiding in Plain Sight* lies in its refusal to provide easy answers. Instead, it opens doors to questions that have haunted humanity for centuries and will undoubtedly follow us into the future: Who are we, truly, when observed from the outside? What are the consequences of our choices when viewed across millennia? And most profoundly, are we prepared for the weight of knowing that we are not alone?

For those who pick up this book, prepare to embark on a journey both outward and inward. *Hiding in Plain Sight* is a rare gift—one that invites you to see yourself not just as a fleeting moment in time but as part of a grander, cosmic story. It is a reminder that in every observation, there is reflection, and in every reflection, there is potential for transformation.

—Zera Schmidt

Author, Philosopher, and Speculative Fiction Enthusiast

Appendices

Appendix A: Key Terms and Concepts

Zepharite High Council: An advanced interstellar governing body tasked with observing and documenting the development of intelligent species across the universe.

Vaelor: A chronicler of the Zepharite High Council, whose mission is to observe humanity without intervention.

The Cloaking Field: Advanced Zepharite technology enabling invisibility and undetectable observation of human activity.

The Anomaly: A recurring term referring to unintentional disruptions caused by Zepharite technology, often influencing human civilizations in unpredictable ways.

The Council Debate: Ongoing deliberations within the Zepharite High Council about whether to intervene in humanity's development or remain passive observers.

Appendix B: Humanity's Pivotal Encounters With The Zepharites

The Cave Hunter's Vision (10,000 BCE): A young hunter in early human history accidentally encounters a cloaked Zepharite observer, inspiring the first myths of divine beings.

The Shaman and the Stars (~3000 BCE): A tribal shaman in early Mesopotamia perceives and interprets the faint shimmer of a Zepharite craft as a spiritual connection to the cosmos.

The Pyramid Engineer (2570 BCE): During the construction of the Great Pyramid of Giza, Imhotep witnesses a cloaked Zepharite drone, influencing his architectural innovations.

The Renaissance Visionary (1485 CE): Leonardo da Vinci experiences an encounter with a Zepharite malfunctioning probe, inspiring his advanced designs for flying machines.

The Codebreaker's Revelation (1941 CE): Clara Morgan, a WWII codebreaker, encounters a technological anomaly, accelerating her breakthroughs in decryption techniques.

Timeline Of Zepharite Observations And Human Milestones

10,000 BCE

Humanity: Early tribes begin developing myths and symbolic representations of the unknown.

Zepharite Observation: A cloaked craft is accidentally discovered by a hunter. The hunter's carvings in his tribe's cave create the earliest depictions of "gods."

2570 BCE

Humanity: Construction of the Great Pyramid of Giza demonstrates advanced engineering and astronomical alignment.

Zepharite Observation: Imhotep witnesses a malfunctioning Zepharite drone during a sandstorm, leading to subtle adjustments in the pyramid's design.

1485 CE

Humanity: Leonardo da Vinci sketches prototypes of flying machines and explores advanced concepts in mechanics and anatomy.

Zepharite Observation: A cloaked atmospheric probe falters in the woods, briefly revealing itself to da Vinci, inspiring new designs.

1941 CE

Humanity: Allied cryptographers crack the Enigma code, significantly influencing the outcome of WWII.

Zepharite Observation: Clara Morgan interprets electromagnetic anomalies caused by a Zepharite malfunction, inspiring new methods in decryption.

2009 CE

Humanity: Bitcoin's genesis marks the beginning of decentralized currency and blockchain technology.

Zepharite Observation: A subtle correction to the blockchain's code stabilizes Satoshi Nakamoto's original system, enabling its scalability.

2027 CE

Humanity: Malik Jafari (Specter) dismantles a global surveillance network using advanced hacking techniques.

Zepharite Observation: Vaelor subtly enhances Malik's algorithms, ensuring success while preserving the illusion of human achievement.

2035 CE

Humanity: The Aurora-1 mission reaches Europa, marking humanity's first exploration of extraterrestrial oceans.

Zepharite Observation: A faint signal from a cloaked Zepharite probe inadvertently reveals mathematical patterns, sparking breakthroughs in Earth's scientific understanding.

2042 CE

Humanity: Athena, an advanced AI, begins assisting in governance, solving global crises.

Zepharite Observation: Fragments of Zepharite logic are embedded in Athena's framework, guiding its ethical evolution.

2058 CE

Humanity: Project Daedalus begins, marking humanity's first attempt at interplanetary colonization on Mars.

Zepharite Observation: Vaelor's chronicles focus on humanity's resilience and the integration of hybrid governance models with Athena's AI.

2062 CE

Humanity: The Celestial Concord establishes a framework for cooperative space exploration and ethical interstellar expansion.

Zepharite Observation: Humanity's progress inspires cautious optimism among the Zepharite High Council, though debates on intervention persist.